First published in Great Britain in 2007 by Buster Books,
an imprint of Michael O'Mara Books Limited,
9 Lion Yard, Tremadoc Road,
London SW4 7NQ

Written by Ellen Bailey
Illustrations by Amanda Enright, Paul Moran
Nellie Ryan and Clive Spong
Edited by Philippa Wingate
Designed by Zoe Quayle
Produced by Joanne Rooke

A CIP catalogue record for this book is available from the British Library.

ISBN: 978-1-906082-16-1

2 4 6 8 10 9 7 5 3 1

Printed and bound in Italy by L.E.G.O.

Papers used by Buster Books are natural, recyclable products made from wood grown in sustainable forests. The manufacturing processes conform to the environmental regulations of the country of origin.

The GIRLS' Treasury

Buster Books

Contents

Horoscope

A   B   C   D

Quizzes

Puzzles

Arts And Crafts

Health And Beauty

All The Answers

It's A Girls' World

There are hundreds of reasons why it's great to be a girl. You have so many fashions to choose from and there are hundreds of hairstyles for you to try. You can experiment with make-up. You can wear skirts OR trousers, or even both at the same time if you want to. Being a girl really is the best of all possible worlds. Plus, of course, you are made of 'sugar and spice and all things nice', while boys are made of 'slugs and snails and puppy dog tails'... or so the rhyme says.

IT'S ALL YOURS

Up there near the top of the list of reasons why it's great to be a girl must be the fact that this book has been written especially for you. Find out how to

have the best friendships, the best bedroom, the best sports moves and the best fun. The book is absolutely packed with cool quizzes, games, activities and fabulous things for you and your friends to enjoy together. Find out how to make paper, fold origami flowers and bake the world's yummiest cookies. Discover what your face shape says about you and scare your friends with a creepy sleepover story.

CELEBRATE

Find out some fascinating facts about what it is like to be a girl in other parts of the world by taking the quiz opposite. Then turn the pages of this book and celebrate all the things that make being a girl so brilliant!

WHERE IN THE WORLD?

Do you know what your sisters around the world are up to? Turn to page 59 to find the answers.

1. Where in the world do girls kiss by rubbing noses when they meet?

a.) Arctic Circle   b.) Brazil
c.) Wales   d.) France

2. Where in the world do girls paint patterns on their hands in henna?

a.) Africa   b.) Australia
c.) Europe   d.) India

3. In which country do girls pledge their allegiance to their country's flag at school?

a.) England   b.) Japan
c.) USA   d.) Scotland

4. In which country do girls do exercises at school every morning before lessons?

a.) China   b.) Italy
c.) Sweden   d.) Germany

5. Where do girls eat salty food before bedtime so they dream about their future husbands?

a.) Hungary   b.) Greece
c.) New Zealand   d.) Greenland

6. Where in the world do girls exchange wooden spoons with their loves on St Valentine's Day?

a.) Wales   b.) Spain
c.) Italy   d.) Mexico

7. In which country does a girl have a huge party when she turns 15, at which her father presents her with her first pair of high heels and dances with her.

a.) Denmark   b.) Greenland
c.) Ireland   d.) Ecuador

8. In which country do girls have special celebrations on their third, fifth and seventh birthdays, because these are thought to be lucky?

a.) Japan   b.) Russia
c.) The Netherlands   d.) Turkey

9. Where in the world do girls get swatted by their boyfriends with a willow branch on Easter Monday, then swat the boys right back on Tuesday?

a.) Poland   b.) Germany
c.) Argentina   d.) England

10. In which country would you see the national costumes shown below?

i.)   ii.)   iii.)   iv.)   v.)

a.) South Africa   b.) Austria   a.) India   b.) Egypt   a.) Spain   b.) Ireland   a.) Sweden   b.) Vietnam   a.) Japan   b.) Mexico

Pet Rescue

It's the summer holidays and you've got a job working at the local pet rescue centre. You've been left in charge, and there's lots to do because some of the pets are misbehaving. Can you complete the puzzles and keep everything in order? You will find all the answers on page 59.

DOG'S DAY

A naughty puppy named Buster has escaped from his kennel. Can you help him find his way back?

BUNNY BUSINESS

Puzzle out the answers to these two questions to find out how to take care of Bubble the bunny.

1. Bubble loves eating carrots. She can eat one carrot every five minutes. How many carrots can she eat in a whole hour?

2. Bubble needs to drink one litre of water every day. Her water bottle only holds 200 millilitres. How many times will you have to refill the bottle in one day?

MATCH MAKER

A lady has come to pick up her kitten, but there are six kittens and they all look very similar. Can you spot the one that matches her photograph below?

COLLECTION CONFUSION

Yikes! Five people have turned up to collect their pets at the same time and there's a bit of confusion. Follow the lines to figure out which pet belongs to which owner.

PETS ON PARADE

Your boss has asked you to arrange the animals into viewing pens. Each row, each column and each of the four different coloured squares must contain a dog, a cat, a rabbit and a fish.

RTSEMHAS 1

EIUPPPS 2

KASENS 3

LSGREBI 4

ENAIGU SGIP 5

TNSETKI 6

MIX UP

Next to each cage at the rescue centre is a sign saying what type of animal is inside. Unfortunately someone has been mixing up the letters. Can you figure out what each sign is meant to say and rearrange the letters so that the animals are spelt correctly?

What's Your Inner Animal?

Answer these questions about your personality and go with the flow to find out which animal you're most like. Then read on to discover what your inner animal can tell you about your personality, your fashion sense and your future career.

I would have a long chat with her and get to the bottom of the problem over ice cream.

. . . meet in a café nearby so that you can chat first about which film to see?

What would you do if your best friend seemed to be upset about something?

I would arrange a fun day out to cheer her up.

START

You and your best friend have planned a trip to the cinema. Do you . . .

I love art. I can't resist being creative!

. . . buy tickets in advance to a film you've been wanting to watch for ages? She'll love it!

What is your favourite subject at school?

Languages. I like the idea of being able to speak with people in foreign countries.

What is your favourite kind of dessert?

I love gooey puddings. The more chocolate and caramel there is the better!

I like delicious, fresh puddings, such as strawberries and cream.

What would be your ideal holiday destination?

I'd like to go somewhere with stunning scenery and beautiful beaches.

I'm drawn to stylish, fast-paced cities, such as Paris, Milan or Los Angeles.

What kind of birthday celebration would you most enjoy?

There's nothing more fun than a night out dancing with friends.

I'd go shopping with a group of friends, and then have dinner in a fancy restaurant.

BUNNY

Bunnies are social animals with lots of love to give. Your friends know they can depend on you, and you're a great listener. You love cozy clothes and look incredible in soft cardigans. Your ideal job would be a teacher or therapist.

BIRD

Just like a bird, you're a free spirit who loves the great outdoors and being at one with nature. You like bohemian clothes and love going bare-foot. You are your own boss and have the creative energy needed to set up your own business.

KITTEN

You're a feisty, kitten-like girl who's the life and soul of every party. You love showing off your figure in the latest fashions and always have your finger on the pulse. You'd be successful in advertising, events management or public relations.

PONY

You're a pony because you're strong minded and know exactly what you want. You're aware of what's in fashion but avoid trends that don't suit you. You can do anything you set your mind to, and would make an excellent lawyer or doctor.

The Strange Case
of the
Spooky School Trip

It's the day before Sarah's birthday and her class are driving to Biverack Castle. They've been driving for hours and are deep in the mountains . . .

THIS PLACE LOOKS REALLY SCARY.

WHY ON EARTH HAVE OUR TEACHERS BROUGHT US HERE?

AT LEAST YOU TWO DON'T HAVE TO SPEND YOUR BIRTHDAY HERE. I DO!

WELCOME TO BIVERACK CASTLE. I'LL TAKE YOU TO YOUR ROOMS. DON'T TOUCH ANYTHING!

BIVERACK CASTLE? LOOKS MORE LIKE *SHIVERACK* CASTLE TO ME!

THAT PAINTING GIVES ME THE CREEPS.

LOOK, IT SAYS:
ELIZABETH CHANTER
1819-1826

SHE MUST HAVE BEEN ONLY SEVEN WHEN SHE DIED.

Later that night . . .

ARGH!
IT'S THE LITTLE GIRL!

WAKE UP YOU TWO, I'VE SEEN A GHOST!

DON'T BE RIDICULOUS, SARAH. GO BACK TO SLEEP.

WELL I CAN'T SLEEP WITH THAT PAINTING LOOKING AT ME. IT'S GOING OUTSIDE THE DOOR.

THIS IS GOING TO BE THE WORST BIRTHDAY I HAVE EVER HAD.

What Does Your Face Shape Say About You?

TRACE YOUR FACE

To find out what shape your face is, pull back your hair and look straight on into a mirror. Take a lipstick and draw around the outline of your head's reflection on the surface of the mirror. Compare the shape you make on the mirror with the shapes shown here. Decide which it most resembles, then read what this says about your personality.

CIRCLE

All the outer points of your face are an equal distance from your nose.

You're a kind, caring girl who is easy to talk to. Your feelings are easily hurt so stay away from people who are less sensitive than you.

TRIANGLE

You have a small forehead leading to a broad chin.

You're a hard worker and everyone admires and respects you. Don't forget to let your hair down every once in a while.

RECTANGLE

You have a broad forehead and a square jaw.

You're a strong-minded girl who knows what she wants and usually gets it. Don't be afraid to show your sensitive side.

HEART

You have a broad forehead leading to a narrow chin.

You're a carefree girl who's not afraid to show her emotions. Remember, not everyone finds it as easy to show their feelings.

OVAL

Your face is taller than it is wide – shaped like an egg.

You are the life and soul of every party and have loads of friends. It's OK to let people know when you're feeling down.

Make-Up Mayhem

Reveal the contents of this make-up bag by colouring in each shape that contains a dot.
For the best result, try to colour in a pen that matches the colour of the dot. You'll find the answers on page 59.

The Sweet Smell Of Success

Answer the questions below and then look at page 59 to find out which type of perfume would best suit your personality.

1. Which of these skirts would you be most likely to wear?

2. Which of these CDs would you be most likely to buy?

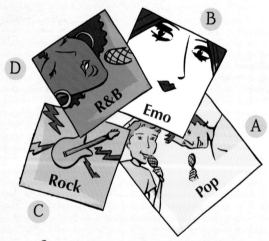

3. Which is your favourite season?

4. You're out for dinner at a restaurant – which of these do you choose?

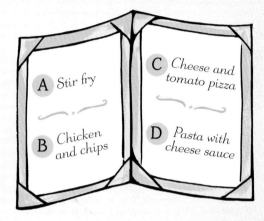

A Stir fry

B Chicken and chips

C Cheese and tomato pizza

D Pasta with cheese sauce

5. Which type of holiday most appeals to you?

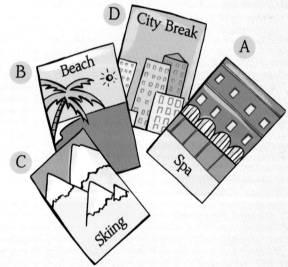

6. Which type of film would you be most likely to rent?

Host A Spa Day

Why not invite your friends round for an afternoon of spa-style luxury and pampering?
Not only will you get to spend the day hanging out, gossiping and sharing beauty secrets,
you'll also finish up feeling completely relaxed and looking absolutely gorgeous. Here's how to do it:

TELL YOUR FRIENDS

Cut out the invites on page 21 and personalise them by completing the pictures on the backs. Send one to each of your friends. The invites include a list of things that your friends will need to bring with them, and a space for you to ask each person for one extra item. If, for example, you know that one of your friends owns curling tongs or a brilliant collection of nail varnishes, then why not ask her to bring those? Ask for anything that will add to the beautification bonanza!

DECORATE THE ROOM

Follow these tips to create a relaxing environment with a back-to-nature feel and health-spa atmosphere.

- Drape white sheets over the furniture.
- Move any green plants in the house into your room.
- Fill small bowls with water and float flower heads in them.
- Put on some calming music. (You could visit your local library to see if they have CDs of rainforest noises or sounds of the sea.)
- Create a gentle lighting effect by turning off the main light and placing lamps or fairy lights around the room.

MAKE SOME SPA-STYLE SNACKS

Choose an area of your room to turn into a small restaurant and stock it with the following healthy snacks:

- Sparkling water and fruit juices
- Fresh fruit
- Nuts and seeds
- Mini sandwiches
- Strawberry and marshmallow kebabs
- Herbal teas

TOP TIP

Keep a camera handy so that you can snap shots of your friends before and after their relaxing afternoon and beauty treatments.

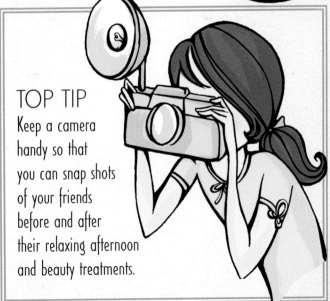

Spa Day Treats

Now that you've got your bedroom looking and feeling like a spa, here are some of the different beauty treatments you can offer to your guests.

MAGICAL MANICURE

Fill a small bowl with warm water and a teaspoon of lemon juice. Place your guest's fingers in the water and leave for five minutes. This removes any discolouration caused by nail polish they have worn in the past. Place a dab of hand cream on each nail and massage in. File nails into an oval shape for a natural look, or a square shape for a more dramatic effect. Carefully paint the nails. Leave them to dry before applying a second coat.

FABULOUS FACIAL

Make a face mask by mixing up one teaspoon of runny honey, three tablespoons of natural yogurt, and a few drops of lemon juice. Wash your guest's face with warm water and then apply the face mask with a paintbrush. Place slices of cucumber over her eyes. Leave for five minutes and then wash off. Splash her face with iced water (this will close the pores in her skin and stop any dirt getting in). Finally, massage some moisturiser into her face.

HEAVENLY HAIR

Gather as many hair bands, slides and other hair accessories as you can find. Take it in turns to create fabulous hair styles for each other.

PERFECT PEDICURES

Create a foot soak by adding a tablespoon of baking soda and a teaspoon of bath oil to a large bowl of warm water. Soak your guest's feet in this for ten minutes to soften her skin and loosen dead skin cells. Take a nail brush and scrub her feet all over. Then dry them and massage in some moisturiser. Place a wad of cotton wool or tissue between each toe to space them out, then apply a layer of nail polish. Allow to dry then apply a second coat.

MUST HAVE MAKE-UP

Apply fabulous, fresh-faced make-up to your guest's cleansed and moisturised skin. Keep tones neutral to enhance her new healthy glow. Don't forget to take your 'after' photos once everyone's had their make-up done. You could even get a few copies printed and give them to your friends to remind them of their super spa day.

I, ...

Invite You,

....

To A Spa Day

At ....

....

Date ....

Time ....

Please bring the following:
- Dressing gown • Flip flops
- Hairband • Face cloth • Mirror
- ....

Get Ready To Be Pampered!

I, ...

Invite You,

....

To A Spa Day

At ....

....

Date ....

Time ....

Please bring the following:
- Dressing gown • Flip flops
- Hairband • Face cloth • Mirror
- ....

Get Ready To Be Pampered!

I, ...

Invite You,

....

To A Spa Day

At ....

....

Date ....

Time ....

Please bring the following:
- Dressing gown • Flip flops
- Hairband • Face cloth • Mirror
- ....

Get Ready To Be Pampered!

I, ...

Invite You,

....

To A Spa Day

At ....

....

Date ....

Time ....

Please bring the following:
- Dressing gown • Flip flops
- Hairband • Face cloth • Mirror
- ....

Get Ready To Be Pampered!

Finish this picture

Give me a gorgeous hair style

Finish this picture

What goes into your smoothie?

Finish this picture

Give me glamorous eye make-up

Finish this picture

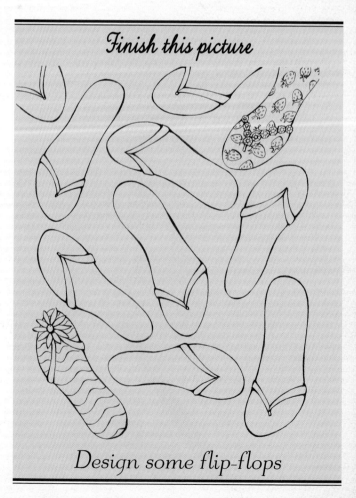

Design some flip-flops

A Scary Sleepover Story

Read this story through again and again, until you know it by heart. Then next time you have your bravest friend over for a sleepover, make sure things go with a BANG. Ahhhhhh!

Gather together the following items: a blindfold, a saucepan half-filled with water and a sponge or dish cloth. At midnight, blindfold your friend and sit her on your bed. Tell her this spine-chilling tale, whispering the words that appear in *italics*, shouting the words that appear in CAPITALS, and acting out the things that are in (brackets).

NOISES IN THE DARK

Once upon a time there was an old, blind lady. She lived with her trusty guide dog, Billy. He was her best friend in the whole world. One day, she and Billy were listening to the news on the radio.

(Speak into your cupped hand.)
"There has been a mysterious series of pet murders in the village. Everyone is advised to lock their doors and windows and not to let their pets go outside until the murderer has been caught."

"How horrible!" said the old lady to Billy. "Let's make sure the doors are locked and then go straight to bed."

(Lead your friend to the door and windows of your bedroom and let her check they are shut.)
Billy led the old lady around the house so that she could check all the locks. Satisfied that they were safe, the old lady got into her night gown, and Billy lay down in his usual position beside her bed.

(Lead your friend back to the bed and lie her down.)
"Good night, Billy," said the old lady, and reached out her hand over the edge of the bed. As always, Billy gave her hand a big, slobbery lick.
(Brush your friend's hand with the wet sponge.)
With that the old lady fell fast asleep. *Shhhhhhh.*

"BILLY!" The old lady woke up with her heart pounding.

(Drip water from the sponge into the saucepan.)
Drip, drip, drip, drip, drip.
"What on earth is that dripping noise, Billy?" asked the old lady. "Did we leave a tap on?" She got out of bed and felt her way towards the bathroom.

(Lead your friend out of your room and into the bathroom. Let her check the taps are turned off.)

"No, the sink taps aren't on," said the old lady, feeling her way around. So she headed back to the bedroom and got into bed.

(Lead your friend back to your room and lie her on the bed. Then leave her there and walk to a corner as far away from her as possible.)

Suddenly the little old lady heard footsteps creeping slowly towards her. Was it Billy?
(Walk towards your friend. When you are beside her breathe on her neck.)

The old lady could feel breath on her neck.
"Billy, is that you?" she whispered.

WOOF!
(Bark really loudly right near your friend's ear and watch as she jumps out of her skin.)

Balance Your Boudoir

Do you have trouble sleeping? Are you finding it difficult to get down to your homework? Does your pocket money seem to disappear the day you get it? Have you been arguing with members of your family? Has it ever occurred to you that the way your bedroom is arranged might be to blame?

FENG SHUI YOUR BEDROOM

Feng Shui is an ancient art practised in China and Japan. It is used to bring people luck, health and happiness. Architects and interior designers use it to create beautiful buildings with peaceful interiors.

❶ Below is an octagon known as the *Pah Kwa*. Place this book on your bedroom floor with the East arrow pointing in the direction that the sun rises.

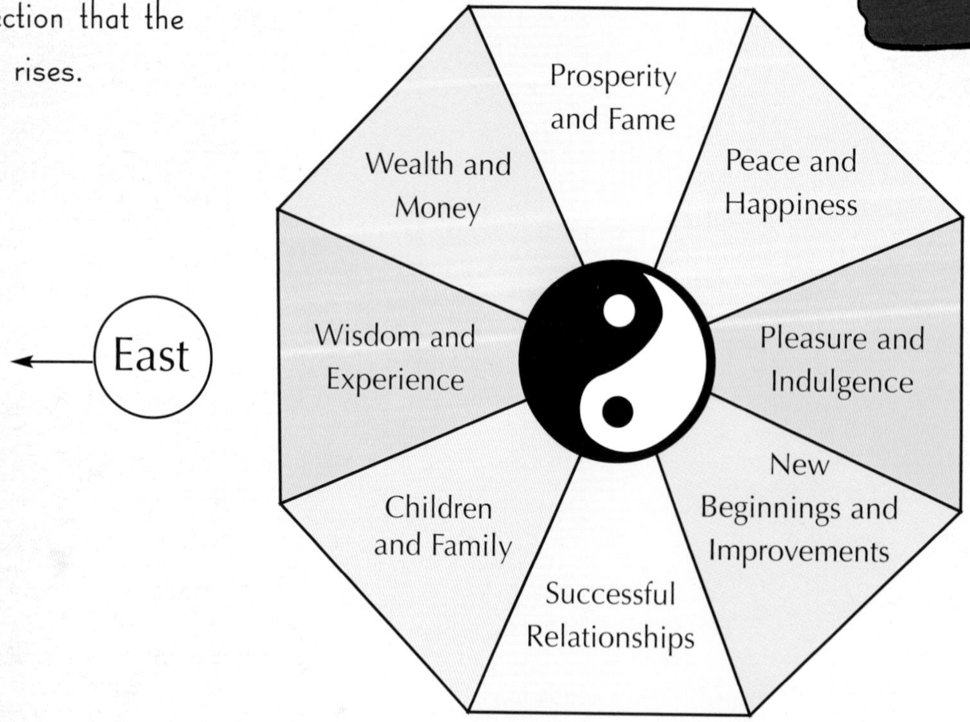

Prosperity and Fame

Wealth and Money

Peace and Happiness

East

Wisdom and Experience

Pleasure and Indulgence

New Beginnings and Improvements

Children and Family

Successful Relationships

❷ Imagine that each of the octagon's sections continues out across your bedroom floor. Each area has a different significance and can help you in a different way.

❸ Rearrange your furniture and belongings so that they are located in sections that match what you use them for. For example, you might want to put your bed in the 'Peace and Happiness' area, your desk in the 'Wisdom and Experience' area, and your piggy bank in the 'Wealth and Money' area.

ENERGISE YOUR LIFE

In *Feng Shui*, the flow of energy is called *Ch'i*. If it moves too fast you may feel tense, too slowly and you may feel lazy. Here's how to improve the flow of *Ch'i* in your room:

❶ Trees and water encourage *Ch'i* to move smoothly. If you can see either from your bedroom window, arrange a mirror so that this view is reflected into the room.

❷ Place a small plant in front of your window to stop the *Ch'i* rushing out.

❸ If you have ceiling beams or other long, straight lines in your room, stop the *Ch'i* darting along them too quickly by tying ribbons round them.

❹ Arrange your furniture diagonally across the corners so that the *Ch'i* doesn't get stuck in them.

❺ Place plants in front of jutting-out corners.

❻ Arrange any chairs so that, when you are sitting on them, you can see who is coming in the door.

GO WITH THE FLOW

Here's a bedroom before and after it has been rearranged with the *Pah Kwa*. Imagine that energy is flowing all around your room. If you run around pretending to be this energy, you'll find that some things, such as clutter, will slow you down. So keep your bedroom as tidy as you can.

BEFORE

AFTER

Origami Bouquet

MAKING THE FLOWER HEAD

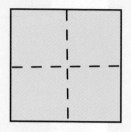

1. Fold the sheet in half from edge to edge in both directions, then unfold it.

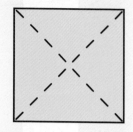

2. Turn it over and fold it in half from corner to corner in both directions, then unfold it.

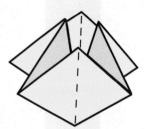

3. Next, fold along creases as shown above.

4. Place the diamond shape in front of you with the open end at the top.

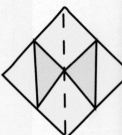

5. Fold the left and right corners of the top layer in to the centre.

6. Then unfold.

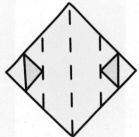

7. Fold the left and right corners in towards the new crease as shown.

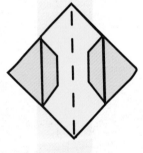

8. Now fold the two sides in towards the centre again as shown.

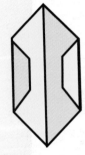

9. Turn the whole thing over and repeat on the other side, so that you end up with this shape.

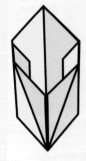

10. Making sure the open end is still at the top, fold the lower edges into the centre line.

11. Turn the whole thing over and repeat this on the other side.

12. Hold the bottom of the tulip with one hand, and gently open the 'flower' with the other hand.

13. You should now have a tulip that looks like this.

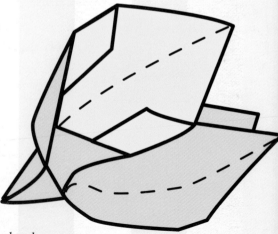

Now it is time to make the stem . . .

MAKING THE FLOWER STEM

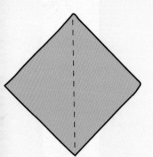

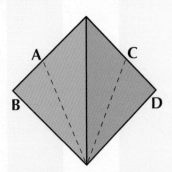

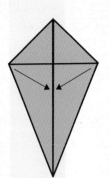

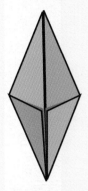

14. Fold the sheet in half from corner to corner, then unfold.

15. Fold the bottom-right and bottom-left edges into the centre line.

16. Then fold the top-right and top-left edges to the centre line to make a diamond shape.

17. Turn the diamond up the other way.

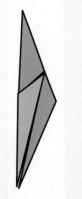

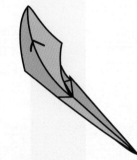

18. Fold in half along the centre crease.

19. Fold the bottom-right edge over to the left edge, then turn over and do the same on the other side.

20. Hold the bottom of the leaf with one hand, and bend back the top with the other.

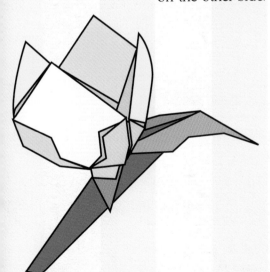

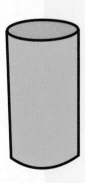

21. Staple the tulip into the centre of the leaf.

22. Glue a strip of brightly coloured wrapping paper around a toilet roll tube to create a vase.

23. Make as many tulips as you like, and place them in the vase.

A Celebration Of Friendship

THE FRIENDSHIP QUIZ

Answer a, b or c to the following questions, then turn to page 60 to find out just what kind of friend you are.

1. Your best friend tells you she's having trouble with her homework. What would you do?

a.) I'd suggest a trip to the cinema to take her mind off it.

b.) I'd organise a study group at which members help each other with the assignment.

c.) I'd talk her through exactly how I did my homework.

2. Which of the following would you be most likely to give your friend on her birthday?

a.) A DVD of her favourite film.

b.) A ticket for a day at a theme park.

c.) That T-shirt she's been admiring for ages.

3. Your friend phones you in tears because she's had an argument with her mum. What would you do?

a.) I would tell her a funny story to cheer her up.

b.) I'd give her practical advice about what I would do if I found myself in the same situation.

c.) I'd listen while she tells me all about the argument.

4. You've gone round to spend the day at your friend's house. What would you do together?

a.) We would bake some delicious cookies.

b.) We'd make up a dance routine to a cool track.

c.) We would have a long chat about school, boys, clothes and make-up.

5. Your friend tries on a top that you don't think suits her. What would you do?

a.) I'd say that the top looks funny, then try something ridiculous on myself to make her laugh.

b.) I'd rush around the shop finding other tops that I think would suit her better.

c.) I'd tactfully explain that I don't think it suits her, and reassure her that everyone looks horrible in that shade of lime green!

6. A girl at school says something mean to your friend. What would you do?

a.) I would think of a clever comeback that makes the mean girl look silly.

b.) I'd tell the girl to stop being so horrible.

c.) I'd take the girl aside and explain that she had hurt my friend's feelings, and ask her not to do it again.

FRIENDSHIP FLOURISHES

'Friendship flourishes' are small gestures designed to remind your best friend how much she means to you.
For a friendship flourish to have its desired effect, it must come when your friend is least expecting it.
Don't wait until her birthday or a special occasion – just choose one of the following flourishes and do it today!

1. Post her a bar of her favourite chocolate.

2. Plant some seeds of her favourite flower in a pretty pot and give them to her as the shoots start to show through.

3. Collect memorabilia from things you do together (train tickets, cinema stubs, photo-booth pictures, etc.) and put them together in a cool collage.

4. Collect the recipes of dishes you think she'll like and paste them into a personalised recipe book.

5. Make her a batch of fairy cakes, spell her name out across them and arrange them in a pretty box.

6. Text her the ringtone of her favourite song.

7. Make her a playlist of her favourite songs.

8. Enter a competition on her behalf – if she wins she'll get a great surprise.

9. Give her an item of your clothing that you know she loves. Next time you are at her house, sneak into her room and leave it on her wardrobe door with a note tied to the hanger saying **'with love from your best friend xx'**.

10. Fill in the certificate below. Then cut it out and present it to your best friend.

Friendship Certificate

This is to certify that

----

is the best friend in the whole world.
The qualities I admire most in her are:

1. ------------------------ 2. ------------------------ 3. ------------------------

We have been friends for --------------- years and --------------- months

The date we met was --

The place we met at was --

The first thing we talked about was --

I promise that we will be best friends for ever and ever.

Signed ------------------------------------ Date ------------------------

Fashion Fun

TERRIBLE TWINS

Laura and Helen are identical twins who get annoyed when their friends can't tell them apart. Spot ten differences between the girls to show that you are worthy of joining their friendship group! Check your answers on page 60.

SHOPPING SPREE

Four friends have gone shopping for new T-shirts. Can you use the clues below to work out the favourite colour of each girl? Fill in their names next to the T-shirt in their favourite colour. Check your answers on page 60.

- *Suzie doesn't like green or blue.*
- *Pippa's top is not pink.*
- *Lisa doesn't like pink or green.*
- *Suzie's top isn't blue or pink.*
- *Kate doesn't like yellow.*

CUSTOMISE A T-SHIRT

Turn a boring old T-shirt into something special with one of these easy customising projects.

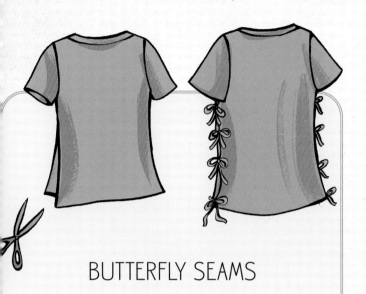

BUTTERFLY SEAMS

Cut along the left and right seams from the bottom of the T-shirt to under the arms. Make four, equally spaced small slits opposite each other along the lines you've just cut. Cut a ribbon into eight 10cm lengths then thread it through the opposite slits, and tie into bows.

PRETTY PUNK

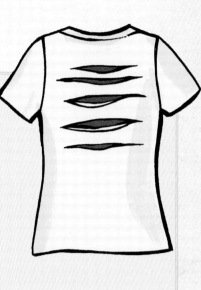

Cut slits across the front of the T-shirt then wear it with a brightly coloured camisole top underneath.

SUPER-COOL STENCIL

Cut a stencil out from a piece of card then pin it onto the T-shirt and paint over it with fabric paints. Remove the stencil and you'll be left with a cool design.

ROMANTIC RIBBONS

Make small slits along the collar, bottom edge and sleeves of a T-shirt. Thread a length of ribbon in and out of the slits along the collar. Tie in a bow at the back. Now do the same around the bottom and around the ends of the sleeves.

FUNKY FRINGE

Use fabric glue to stick a lace fringe around the sleeves and bottom of the T-shirt.

~ JUST FOR GIRLS ~

Green Sisters

Being green is all about looking after the planet. It's about protecting the environment and keeping our forests, seas, rivers and wildlife safe from harm. It's important that everyone does their bit to help.

DOING IT FOR THE WORLD

Answer the quiz questions below, then turn to page 60 to find out just how green you are.

1. How do you usually get to school?

a.) I either walk or cycle.

b.) I take the train or a bus.

c.) I always get a lift all the way there in a car.

2. How much of your household waste is recycled?

a.) Everything that can be and we have a composter.

b.) The bottles and newspapers, but not much else.

c.) What is recycling?

3. When you have finished watching TV in the evening what do you do?

a.) I always turn the TV off at the plug on the wall.

b.) I switch the TV off with the remote control.

c.) I usually leave the TV on for the next person.

4. When you go food shopping how do you carry everything home?

a.) In a strong bag I take with me every time I go.

b.) In old plastic carrier bags from other shops.

c.) In new plastic bags provided by the supermarket.

5. How often do you get a new mobile phone?

a.) I've had the same one for years.

b.) Once a year.

c.) Every time a cool new design comes out.

6. What kind of holiday did you last go on?

a.) I had a UK-based holiday.

b.) I took a trip in Europe.

c.) I flew halfway around the world by plane.

MAKE A GREEN HOME

Here are some things to cut out and stick around your
house to remind your family to be green.

Save energy by sticking these reminders next
to any plugs that should be switched off when
the appliance is not in use.

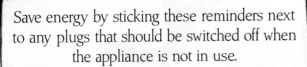

Turn me off!	Turn me off!	Turn me off!
Turn me off!	Turn me off!	Turn me off!
Turn me off!	Turn me off!	Turn me off!
Turn me off!	Turn me off!	Turn me off!
Turn me off!	Turn me off!	Turn me off!

Help conserve water by sticking this up
next to your toilet to remind everyone
not to rush to flush!

If it's brown
Flush it down.
If it's yellow
Let it mellow.

Lots of kitchen and garden waste can be
turned into compost. Get a separate bin in
your kitchen then put this sign up to remind
everyone which things can be composted.

Encourage shops to sell greener products
by getting your family to agree to the
shopping contract below. Cut it out and
stick it on your fridge.

✓ Tea bags
✓ Vegetable peelings
✓ Leftover vegetables
✓ Leftover fruit
✓ Egg shells
✓ Hedge trimmings
✓ Old plants
✓ Grass cuttings
✓ Hay and straw
✓ Hair cuttings

✗ Meat
✗ Cheese
✗ Fish
✗ Boys!

FAMILY SHOPPING CONTRACT

• **We will buy our food from local shops
to save on petrol.**

• **We will resist products that have been
flown around the world. Instead we will
buy local fruit and vegetables at the time
of year that they naturally grow.**

• **We will choose organic foods farmed
without the use of chemicals that are
harmful to the earth.**

• **We will avoid products that come
in lots of wasteful packaging.**

Finish The Flowers

Do you have green fingers? Fill this box with fabulous flowers and shade them in vibrant colours.

Make Your Own Paper

YOU WILL NEED

- ✓ • an old washing-up bowl
- ✓ • masking tape
- ✓ • a pair of old, thin tights
- ✓ • old newspapers
- ✓ • a large mixing bowl
- ✓ • water
- ✓ • a wire coat hanger
- ✓ • PVA glue

1. The first thing you need to do is to make a frame. Carefully undo the coat hanger, bend it into a square and tape up the rough ends.

2. Next you need to stretch one leg of the tights over the coat hanger. Tie a knot at either end so that the tights are pulled taut across the coat hanger.

3. Tear a few pages of newspaper into small squares about 3 cm by 3 cm in size.

4. Add the torn paper to a large bowl containing about three cups of water. Use your hands to squeeze and tear the paper in the water until it becomes a grey pulp.

5. Fill the washing-up bowl with 13 cm of water and add three tablespoons of PVA glue (get permission first!). Add the grey pulp and mix it all well.

6. Take your coat hanger frame, and scoop it into the bowl and under the mixture. Lay it on the bottom of the bowl and spread the pulp evenly over it. Now slowly lift the frame out of the sink.

7. All you need to do now is leave the frame in a warm place, perhaps in the airing cupboard or outside if it is a nice day. When it is dry, simply peel off your sheet of paper from the frame.

Super Sport Skills

HOW TO ROLLER SKATE BACKWARDS

1. The best position for skating backwards is to stand with your arms held out either side like wings and your knees slightly bent. This helps your balance. Keep your body upright and don't look down at your feet.

2. At first it is a good idea to hold on to a friend to help you balance (find one who can skate well). Place your feet in a 'V' shape with your toes together and your heels apart. Get your friend to push you gently backwards. As you start to move, straighten your knees slightly and push your left leg out to the side and then in again. See how far you can travel by repeating this movement. Do the same with your right leg.

3. Next try moving both legs together. Get your friend to push you back, then keep your weight equal over both legs and push both legs out to the side and then back to the centre.

4. Practice this until you can start moving backwards without the help of your friend. You can now roller skate backwards!

HOW TO CONTROL A HOCKEY BALL

1. To push a hockey ball, you need to use the flat edge of the 'toe' of your stick.

2. If you are right-handed, your left hand should be near the top of the stick. Hold the stick as if you are shaking hands with it. Make a 'V' shape with your thumb and forefinger, so your thumb points down towards the toe of your stick.

3. Your right hand should grasp the stick in the same way, about half way down. Keep the palm of your right hand against the back of the stick so you can guide it forward.

4. Practise swinging the stick backwards and forwards, and if necessary adjust the position of your hands so they feel comfortable.

5. Now try pushing the ball, gently at first. Use your left hand to control the stick and your right hand to give force to your stroke. Turn your body and point your left shoulder in the direction you want the ball to go. Keep practising until you develop excellent ball control.

HOW TO PLAY ULTIMATE FRISBEE

Ultimate Frisbee is a fabulous, fast-paced team game to play with a gang of friends. Divide into two teams of players – ideally there should be seven on each team. You will then need to mark out a pitch. It should be rectangular, and either end should have a goal-scoring area called the 'endzone'. The measurements below show the size of a tournament-size pitch, but you can make yours smaller to fit the space you are playing in, just keep the pitch in the same proportions.

The aim of the game is to score goals by passing the frisbee to a team member who is standing within the opposing team's endzone. The first team to score ten goals is the winner.

To begin, each team should line up on their endzone line. Decide which team will start with the frisbee. That team is the 'defence' and should start by throwing the frisbee to the other team (the 'offence').

After each goal the teams swap ends and play begins again with each team lined up on their endzone line. The team that just scored starts with the frisbee and begins play again by throwing it to the opposing team.

RULES

*   You cannot run with the frisbee.
*   You can't hold the frisbee for more than ten seconds before passing it on.
*   If the frisbee hits the ground, is thrown outside the pitch, or is intercepted, then play passes to the opposing team, and that team becomes the 'offence'.
*   No physical contact is allowed between players. Physical contact results in a foul, and play passes to the team that was fouled.
*   Players must observe the spirit of the game – play fairly and with respect for the other team.
*   Have fun!

The dimensions shown below are of a tournament-sized Ultimate Frisbee pitch.
You can make yours smaller to fit the space you are playing in.

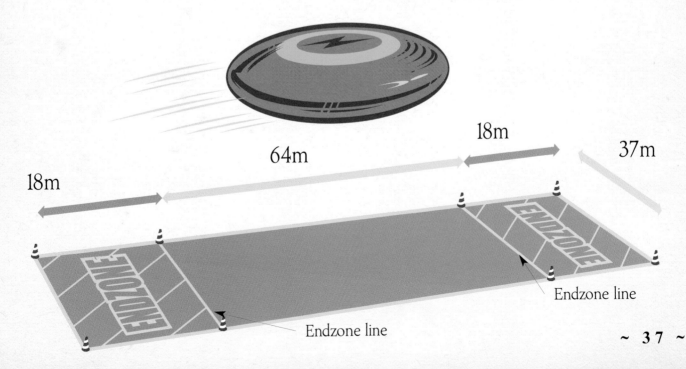

18m   64m   18m   37m

Endzone line

Endzone line

A Costume Drama

"I've got some great news," Lucy shrieked at her friends Emma and Chloe, before she'd even sat down in her school chair that morning. "They're filming the costume drama *Smiles And Sunshine* at our school today, and my aunt is the director. We have to go to the set at lunchtime. That gorgeous boy Jack Finlay is in it. If I get a starring role, he's bound to notice me."

"But we're decorating our outfits for the school's summer party at lunch," Chloe protested.

"Yes we are," Emma chipped in. "We're going to the art room to use fabric paints. I know you've found your dress, but we don't have anything to wear yet and the party's in two days' time."

"In any case, the school hasn't said anything about a film crew, or Jack Finlay," added Chloe. The girls knew Lucy often stretched the truth, so they took her claims with a pinch of salt.

LUCY STAMPS HER FOOT

"You two are such pains in the neck," said Lucy with a scowl. "This could be my one and only chance of finding stardom, and it's going to be ruined because you don't have stupid outfits for the summer party. You won't make anything as lovely as my new red dress," Lucy continued. "Why can't you play about with fabric paint tomorrow?"

"The art room is only open on a Thursday," said Chloe bravely. Emma and Chloe stared awkwardly at their shoes. Once Lucy was annoyed, her mood could last all day.

"Why don't you go to the film set anyway, Lucy?" Chloe suggested as the bell rang for lunch.

"It won't be so much fun if you can't see me all dressed up and stealing the show," said Lucy, as she got up sulkily from her desk. "But, if you insist on going to the art room, I'll go and get our bags."

When Lucy returned a few minutes later she seemed calmer.

"Phew! I was worried we had a Mean, Mad Lucy mood on our hands," Emma whispered to Chloe with relief.

"Me too," said Chloe. "Anyway there's no chance the film will give school girls like us a role."

The three girls walked away from their classroom across the path that led to the art room. Then, suddenly, Lucy stopped dead in her tracks.

"Let's go this way," she said with a mysterious smile. Both girls knew it was quicker to turn left to the art room, but they didn't say anything and followed Lucy.

WHAT A TRANSFORMATION

When they reached the school hall Emma and Chloe couldn't believe their eyes. The whole building had been transformed into a film set with men and women dressed head to toe in period costume.

"Isn't it amazing," grinned Lucy. "Look, there's my aunt. I'm going to get myself a starring role!" Lucy rushed up to a blonde-haired lady who was holding a clipboard and tapped her on the back.

"Hello Aunt Lydia," Lucy said with a sickly sweet smile.

"I would like to be in your film. I'm a great actress and get all the main parts in school plays. One day I'll be famous."

"Lucy, what are you doing?" gasped Chloe in embarrassment.

"Ssssh!" said Lucy impatiently. "This is my aunt. She has promised to make me a star."

A BIG SURPRISE

"I think we have the perfect part for you, Lucy," said Aunt Lydia with a knowing smile. "And what about you two? Would you like to be in the film too?" she said to Chloe and Emma.

"That would be wonderful," said Emma.

"Thank you," gushed Chloe, astonished.

"This is our wardrobe lady, Martha," said Aunt Lydia beckoning over a flamboyantly dressed lady. "She will fit you out with costumes." Aunt Lydia whispered something to Martha. Then the girls were whisked away to the classroom next door. It was brimming with beautiful dresses, hats and rows of shoes.

"I told you this was a good idea," said Lucy smugly.

"Chloe and Emma, try these dresses on," said Martha, holding up the most beautiful two dresses the girls had ever seen. "Emma, this is yours," Martha waved a pale pink dress, complete with ribbon sash and puffed sleeves. "And Chloe, this one's for you," Martha handed Chloe a striking blue dress with a floating cream underskirt.

"The two of you are playing the Armstrong sisters," said Martha with a look of admiration. "You are very lucky indeed."

"Lucy, this is your outfit. You are playing a servant girl," said Martha taking down a plain grey and white dress. "But..." Lucy was so shocked that for once she couldn't speak a single word.

Emma and Chloe stepped carefully into their dresses. They could barely contain their excitement at wearing such delicate gowns. When Lucy emerged from the classroom she was wearing the ugliest of dresses and the most miserable of faces. Chloe and Emma shot each other little smiles, but tried not to show their delight. "Lucy, you will scrub the steps outside the hall, while Chloe and Emma walk out of the hall and across the lawn with their elder brother, Charles," Martha explained. "Why do they get to walk with Charles?" wailed Lucy. Chloe and Emma realised why Lucy was so annoyed when a tall, handsome boy appeared beside them.

GORGEOUS JACK

"Emma, Chloe, this is Jack Finlay. He will be playing Charles," said Aunt Lydia. The gorgeous Jack Finlay. The girls could not believe their luck.

"Pleased to meet you," said Jack with a gentlemanly nod. "You both look fantastic."

After they had rehearsed their walk with Jack several times, filming began, and the cameras started to roll. As they walked out across the lawn with Jack by their side, Chloe and Emma felt like the luckiest two girls in the world. And all the while, poor Lucy was on her knees scrubbing the hall steps, barely in shot of the cameras at all. "Girls, because you were such good actresses I will let you keep your dresses," said Martha patting them each on the back when the filming stopped.

"Well, I don't want the old rag I had to wear, so you can keep it," grumbled Lucy, tugging at her dress.

"We can wear our dresses to the summer ball," Chloe whispered to Emma as they changed back into their school uniforms.

"I can't wait to see the film," said Emma. Then, suddenly, they heard a voice: "Emma, Chloe, I just wanted to say you did a great job in the film." They swung round to see Jack Finlay. Chloe and Emma blushed with pride before waving Jack goodbye and stepping back into their classroom.

HAPPILY EVER AFTER...

All the girls at Heatherley School were green with envy when Emma and Chloe told them how they had met Jack Finlay that lunchtime. And at the summer party the two girls made such an elegant entrance that even Lucy had to admit they cut a fine figure. When *Smiles And Sunshine* hit the cinemas, the two girls watched with overwhelming excitement for their scene. They agreed that maybe Lucy's idea about becoming famous wasn't such a bad one after all.

~ JUST FOR GIRLS ~

Sussed At School

DISCOVER YOUR LEARNING STYLE

The way you handle everyday situations reveals a lot about your learning style. Follow this flowchart and discover the best way for you to approach your schoolwork.

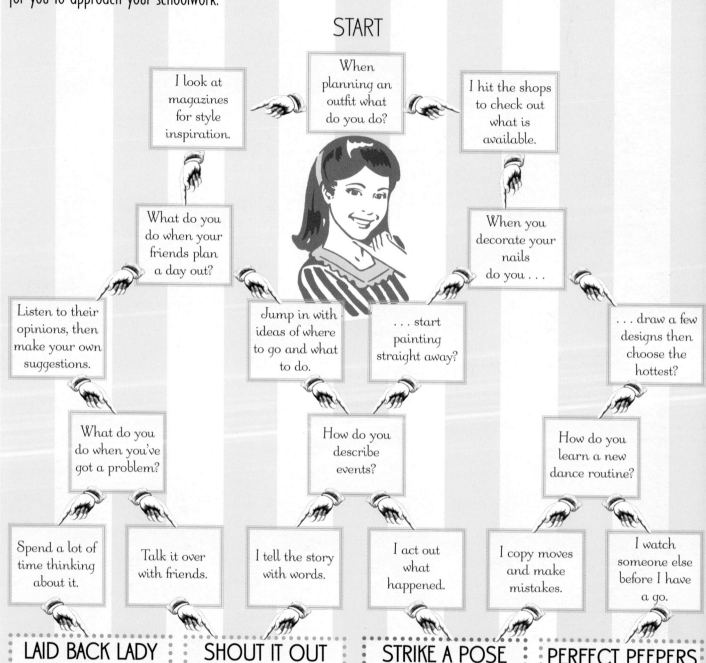

LAID BACK LADY
You find it easiest to remember new information when you have time to think it over. Take ten minutes at the end of each day to look back at your work and you'll find it will all sink in.

SHOUT IT OUT
You understand things best when you hear them or see them written down. Try writing summaries of your work in your own words.

STRIKE A POSE
You find it easiest to learn in hands-on lessons. Why not form a homework group where you and your friends can discuss and explain ideas to each other?

PERFECT PEEPERS
You learn best when there are images for you to look at. Draw diagrams and flowcharts whenever possible and try colour co-ordinating your homework notes.

GET TO SCHOOL

It's Zoe's first day at a new school, but she doesn't know how to get there. Can you help her find her way? The answer is on page 60.

SCHOOL REPORT

Slip these words into conversations with your teachers and they will be seriously impressed. The words might just turn up in your next school report!

- **Pulchritudinous** (means beautiful)
- **Prepossessing** (means attractive)
- **Sagacious** (means wise)
- **Perspicacious** (means insightful)
- **Adroit** (means skilful)

HOW TO GET NOTICED AT SCHOOL

In a large school with loads of pupils it's easy to become just another anonymous girl in uniform. Here are some things you could do to make sure that you stand out from the crowd and that everybody knows your name.

Start your own club and get other kids signed up (find out how on the following page).

Get a group of friends together and ask people to sponsor you for a charity event such as a fun run.

Organise a charity event such as a dance competition. Ask local shops if they will donate some prizes.

If you are brave enough, offer to help the best-looking boy with his homework. He needs friends, too.

Wear your hair in a different style every day of the week. People will soon take note.

Here's a simple one that's guaranteed to work – smile and say hello to everyone whenever you enter a room.

Start A Club

Everyone loves a girl who can keep her friends entertained. If you're looking for something special to do in your spare time, then perhaps it's time to take charge and start your very own club. Whether you have a passion for fashion, are fanatical about films, or if you can't stop cooking, a club is the perfect way for you to share your interests, swap ideas, and have fun. Here's a step-by-step guide how to do it.

1. GETTING STARTED

The first thing to do is talk the idea over with your friends, and see what kind of club you want to form. Everyone's bound to have loads of great ideas and your job will be putting them together to create a club that you're all really excited about. You should also decide if there are going to be any club rules.

2. CHOOSING A NAME

You need to pick a name for your club. It should be catchy and reflect the club's purpose. You could also get the most artistic club member to design a logo and customise club belongings. Various retailers will print designs onto T-shirts, mugs or bags – or you could have a go yourself with some fabric pens.

3. YOUR FIRST MEETING

At the first meeting you should get everyone to read out the following oath:

I do solemnly promise to obey the rules of _____ _____ (name of club). I will never reveal the secret password, or tell anyone about anything discussed during meetings. The club's private business will remain private. I will help my fellow club members whenever they are in need, and will do everything I can to make this the best club ever.

Next, agree a secret password. Then cut out and distribute the membership cards on the next page. Don't forget to design and draw a picture that represents your club (called a logo) on the back of each card.

4. EXPANDING THE CLUB

Why restrict your club's membership to just a few of your close friends? You should try to expand and get as many members as you can. It's a great way to meet new people and make new friends. A sensible place to start is with kids in your class or with members' brothers and sisters. It's a good ideas to let everyone join in, because your club will be so cool that everyone wants to be a member.

Membership Card
Name:
....
Date of Birth:
....
Membership Number:
....
Place your photo here.

Membership Card
Name:
....
Date of Birth:
....
Membership Number:
....
Place your photo here.

Membership Card
Name:
....
Date of Birth:
....
Membership Number:
....
Place your photo here.

Membership Card
Name:
....
Date of Birth:
....
Membership Number:
....
Place your photo here.

Membership Card
Name:
....
Date of Birth:
....
Membership Number:
....
Place your photo here.

Membership Card
Name:
....
Date of Birth:
....
Membership Number:
....
Place your photo here.

Membership Card
Name:
....
Date of Birth:
....
Membership Number:
....
Place your photo here.

Membership Card
Name:
....
Date of Birth:
....
Membership Number:
....
Place your photo here.

DRAW YOUR OWN LOGO

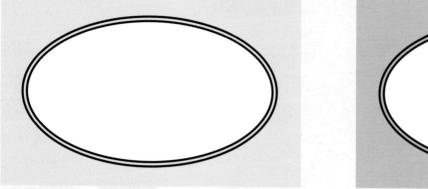

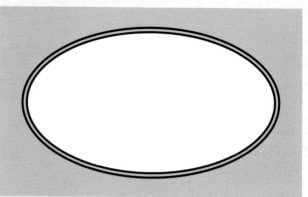

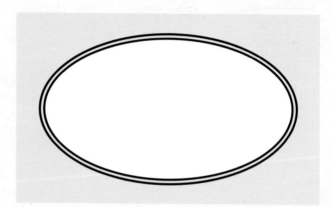

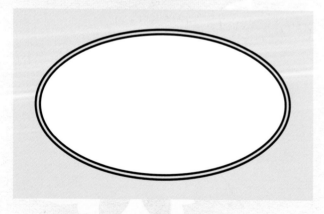

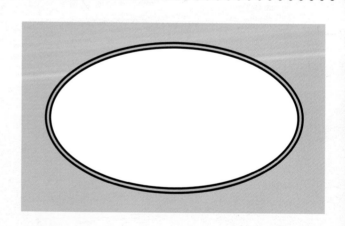

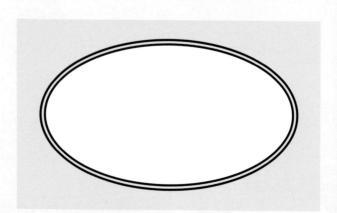

Party Time

It's your best friend's birthday tomorrow and you've been given the job of organising a surprise party. Can you find all the things on the shopping list in the picture below. You will find the answers on page 61.

You will find the answers on page 61.

Shopping List:

- a card with a heart on it
- pink flowery wrapping paper
- a pearl necklace
- a pair of green jeans
- 'Happy Birthday' banner
- a chocolate birthday cake
- pink candles for the cake
- CD of party hits
- a yellow, ziz-zag party hat
- two large boxes of chocolates
- a pink T-shirt with a heart on it
- shoes with bows on them

Daisy's Delicious Dainties

FUNKY FASHIONS

Happy Birthday

Handbag Bingo

1. Handbag bingo is a game for three players. Imagine you are all going on a shopping trip, but one player has forgotten her handbag and needs to borrow items from the others' handbags. Choose which of you will be the 'Forgetter'.

2. The two 'handbag players' then choose either the green handbag and counters or the pink bag and counters. They should cut out the handbag board and the counters.

3. Without letting the Forgetter see, the two handbag players choose nine of their twelve counters and place them all face up on the squares on their game boards.

4. The Forgetter then calls out in a random order the items from the list below that they would like to borrow.

5. Each time the Forgetter says the name of an item that one of the handbag players has on their game board, that player hands the item to the Forgetter.

6. The first person to give the Forgetter all the items from their game board is the winner.

1. Lipstick
2. Nail file
3. Mobile phone
4. Tissues
5. Hairbrush
6. Address book
7. Diary
8. Mints
9. Hair band
10. Magazine
11. Umbrella
12. Chocolate
13. MP3 player
14. Bottle of water
15. Book
16. Mascara
17. Hairspray
18. Moisturiser
19. Compact mirror
20. Personal games console
21. Money
22. Friendship bracelet
23. Pen
24. Notebook

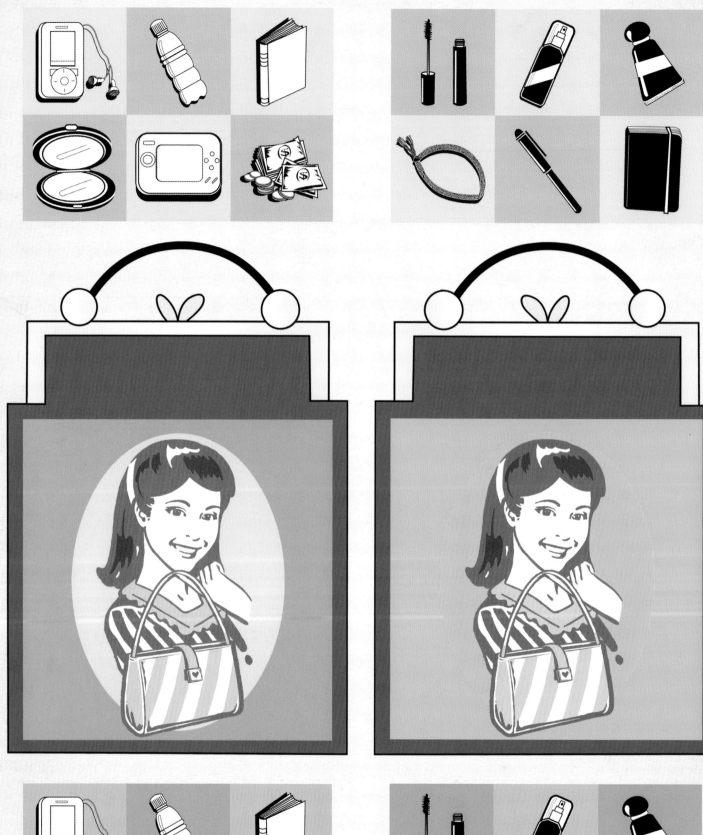

Candy Cookies

These are quite possibly the most delicious cookies you'll ever taste. What is more, they're super-speedy and easy to make.

1. Heat the oven to 190°C/Gas mark 5.

> **Warning**
> Don't risk burnt fingers.
> Get help each time you use the oven.

2. Place the butter and sugar in a bowl and beat together with a wooden spoon. Then stir in the egg and vanilla essence.

INGREDIENTS

115g (4oz) unsalted butter (get this out of the fridge an hour before you start cooking so that it's nice and soft)

200g (7oz) caster sugar

1 egg

1½ tsp vanilla essence

240g (8½oz) plain flour

½ tsp baking powder

¼ tsp salt

250g chocolate chips or sugar-coated chocolate in an assortment of bright colours.

3. Sift the plain flour, baking powder and salt into another bowl and stir them together.

4. Pour the flour mixture into the butter and sugar mixture. Add in the chocolate, and stir everything together.

5. Roll the mixture into golf-ball sized portions. Flatten them with your fingers onto a non-stick baking tray 5cm apart.

6. Bake for 11 minutes. Use oven gloves to carefully remove them from the oven. Don't worry if they don't seem to be quite done – they will harden up as they cool.

7. Place the cookies on a wire rack to cool for ten minutes. If you can resist eating them straight away, you'll find they're even more chewy and delicious after a couple of days.

Paper Crafts

Here is a crafty way of saving the planet. Recycle unwanted wrapping paper, old magazines and newspapers by using them to complete one of these fun projects.

LIGHT UP YOUR LIFE

Instantly brighten up your bedroom by making a dozen of these easy-to-make paper lanterns and stringing them from one corner of the room to another.

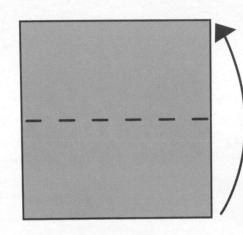

1. Glue two sheets of wrapping paper together back-to-back, pattern side outermost. Fold in half as shown.

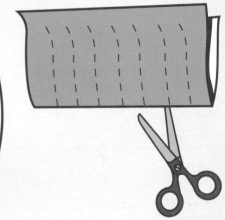

2. Starting at the fold, cut evenly spaced slits into the paper, stopping about 2cm from the end.

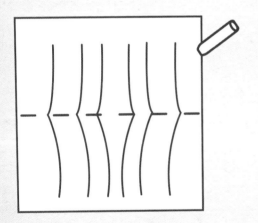

3. Open the piece of paper up again, and put a line of glue along the right-hand edge.

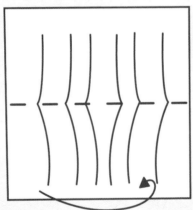

4. Pick up the left-hand edge of the paper, and roll it over so that the left-hand edge meets the line of glue on the right.

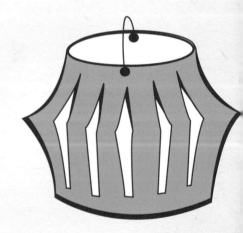

5. Stand the lantern upright and carefully pierce two holes opposite each other into the top and attach a piece of string as shown.

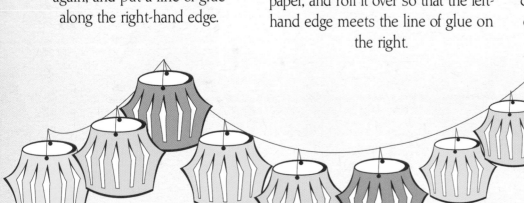

BEAUTIFUL BUTTERFLIES

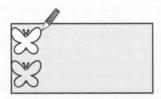

2. In the right-hand corner of the piece of glued wrapping paper draw around the butterfly stencil. Then draw another below. Make sure the left-hand wings are touching the edge of the page. Remove the stencil.

3. Fold the paper in a concertina underneath the butterfly, making sure that the wings go slightly over the edge of each fold.

1. Glue two sheets of wrapping paper back to back, pattern outermost. Set them aside for the glue to dry. Trace over this picture of a butterfly, and cut out the shape to make a stencil.

4. Cut around the butterfly shapes, leaving the folded edges at the tip of the top wings intact. Open up your butterfly chains.

COLOURFUL COLLAGE

Begin by drawing the outline of a picture on a piece of paper. Starting with the background, and building up your picture layer by layer, stick scraps of an old magazine or old scraps of wrapping paper (or even material) into position.

Even a very simple picture can look fantastic when you start building up the different layers.

For the best results match the texture and pattern of the paper to the item in the picture that you're using it for. You could, for example, use silver foil to look like rain, news print to look like a newspaper, and brown paper to look like a parcel.

What Is Your Story?

Here's a romantic tale, but it is incomplete. It's up to you to finish the tale by choosing a, b or c at each stage of the story. Turn to page 61 to find out what your choices reveal about your personality.

Once upon a time there was a young girl from a very poor family. They lived together in . . .

a.) . . . an abandoned castle surrounded by a moat.

b.) . . . a house in the woods that they had made from trees.

c.) . . . a small village by a river.

On the day of her birth, the girl had been visited by an old woman dressed in rags. The woman said that the girl's mother had been very kind to her. In return she would cast a spell that would . . .

a.) . . . give her riches beyond her wildest dreams.

b.) . . . make everybody love her.

c.) . . . always keep her safe from harm.

As the girl grew up, word spread that she was incredibly talented at . . .

a.) . . . fighting enemies.

b.) . . . looking after people.

c.) . . . creating magic potions.

On the girl's twelfth birthday, she received a letter from the king. The letter said that the king had heard about the girl's extraordinary talents, and that he would like her help to . . .

a.) . . . defeat a rival king who was terrorising the land.

b.) . . . defeat a dragon who was stealing children from the land.

c.) . . . defeat a wizard who was threatening to flood the land.

The girl knew that she must go to help the king. She said goodbye to her family, and set off with a spare set of clothes, a packed lunch, and . . .

a.) . . . a sword that had been given to her by her grandfather.

b.) . . . a tin of happiness cookies.

c.) . . . a bag of magical beads.

On arrival at the king's palace the girl was met by a handsome prince. He was very worried about the terrible situation, but overjoyed to see the young girl whom he had heard so much about. The girl and the handsome prince decided to . . .

a.) . . . fight the enemy together.

b.) . . . welcome the enemy to the land in the hope that it would stop causing havoc.

c.) . . . cast a spell that would get rid of the enemy.

Their plan worked and the king was so overjoyed that he threw a huge party in their honour. He invited the girl's family to come and live in his castle, and they all lived there together happily ever after.

The End

It's Written In Your Stars

ARIES, MARCH 21st - APRIL 20th

Confident and energetic, you are always full of enthusiasm and have a great lust for life. You love keeping active and do well at team sports. However, you have been known to boast about your many victories, and to get impatient with your friends when they can't keep up. Try to remember that not everyone has as much get-up-and-go as you.

TAURUS, APRIL 21st - MAY 21st

You are an ambitious lady who knows what she wants and is determined to get it. You love shopping, partying, long bubble baths and indulgence of any kind. Your friends think of you as loyal and affectionate, but be careful not to let your jealous streak push them away.

GEMINI, MAY 22nd - JUNE 21st

Your friendly manner and fun-loving nature mean that you find it easy to make new friends. You get on well with different kinds of people and you are never lost for words. It's important for you to keep active as you get bored easily and can become restless.

CANCER, JUNE 22nd - JULY 23rd

You're a kind and sympathetic girl who enjoys looking after people. Your friends know they can turn to you if ever they have a problem. You are romantic, imaginative and emotional. You feel things very deeply and sometimes get moody, but try not to take it out on others.

LEO, JULY 24th - AUGUST 23rd

Confident, extroverted and charming, you love nothing more than being the centre of attention. You are a natural leader and everyone who meets you admires and respects you. You are generous and caring, but can sometimes be rude to people who don't meet your high standards.

VIRGO, AUGUST 24th - SEPTEMBER 23rd

You are a hard worker who always strives for perfection. Everything – from your school work and bedroom, to your clothing and make-up – is neat, tidy and ordered. You're a modest girl who never boasts, but you can be a bit fussy. Try not to criticise your friends for being less perfect than you.

LIBRA, SEPTEMBER 24th - OCTOBER 23rd

You're an impressive girl who charms everyone she meets. You have a strong sense of right and wrong, and you always make sure things are fair. You're intelligent and good at explaining your ideas and opinions. You do sometimes get angry, so watch your temper.

SCORPIO, OCTOBER 24th - NOVEMBER 22nd

You love learning new things, and your curiosity about everyone and everything means you're rarely bored. When you start a project you are very focused and always see things through to the end. You can sometimes be a little secretive and possessive, so don't forget to share all your amazing discoveries with your friends.

SAGITTARIUS, NOVEMBER 23rd - DECEMBER 21st

Energetic and fun-loving, you enjoy travelling to new places and trying new things. You're funny, generous and open-hearted, and make a great friend. You sometimes make decisions without really thinking them through – so don't just assume things will always work out for the best, or you might end up in trouble.

CAPRICORN, DECEMBER 22nd - JANUARY 20th

You're a trustworthy girl who takes her responsibilities very seriously. Your friends know that if they tell you a secret it will never go any further. You are ambitious, patient and work hard for the things that you want. However it is important that you remember it's OK to let your hair down and have fun every once in a while.

AQUARIUS, JANUARY 21st - FEBRUARY 19th

You're a creative girl who's always brimming with new ideas. You've got a million interesting things to say and frequently stay up into the early hours chatting with friends. You sometimes find it difficult to make decisions and will often change your mind, which can make it harder for you to get things done.

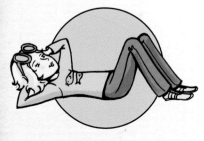

PISCES, FEBRUARY 20th - MARCH 20th

Affectionate, funny and honest, you have a close group of good friends. You're a romantic girl who likes nothing better than spending time daydreaming on your own. You should be careful not to let people take advantage of your kind and generous nature, but also don't exaggerate situations in your head and think this is happening when it's not.

Forty Things Every Girl Should Do In Her Lifetime

Cross off each item as you achieve it. Don't worry, you have got a lifetime to do them all.

1 Cook a gourmet three-course meal.

2 Dye your hair.

3 Make a major fashion mistake.

4 Attend a film premiere.

5 Milk a cow.

6 Learn another language.

7 Win a trophy.

8 Invent a new word.

9 Write a song.

10 Go on holiday with your best friend.

11 Start a blog.

12 Go on a protest march.

13 Help save the planet.

14 Send a message in a bottle.

15 Build a tree house.

16 Get sponsored for charity.

17 Act in a play.

18 Grow something edible from a seed, then eat it.

19 Start a collection.

20 Make a time capsule.

21 Start a new trend.

22 Train a dog.

23 Jump off the top board at the pool.

24 Go ice skating.

25 Complete a crossword.

26 Eat a meal with chopsticks.

27 Keep a diary.

28 Knit a jumper (or at least a scarf for a doll).

29 Perform a magic trick.

30 Develop a party piece.

31 Write a poem.

32 Use a secret code.

33 Host a sleepover.

34 Get an 'A' grade at school.

35 Get an 'E' grade at school.

36 Jump shoot a basketball.

37 Learn to touch-type.

38 Learn to speed-read.

39 Draw a comic strip.

40 Build your own website.

All The Answers

WHERE IN THE WORLD? (PAGE 9)

1.	a	6.	a	10. i.	b
2.	d	7.	d	ii.	a
3.	c	8.	a	iii.	a
4.	a	9.	a	iv.	b
5.	b			v.	a

PET RESCUE (PAGES 10 AND 11)

DOG'S DAY

BUNNY BUSINESS

1. Twelve carrots   2. Refill Bubble's bottle five times.

MATCH MAKER   6

COLLECTION CONFUSION

A = 1, B = 2, C = 3, D = 5, E = 4

MIX UP

1 = HAMSTERS, 2 = PUPPIES, 3 = SNAKES,
4 = GERBILS, 5 = GUINEA PIGS, 6 = KITTENS

PETS ON PARADE

MAKE-UP MAYHEM (PAGE 17)

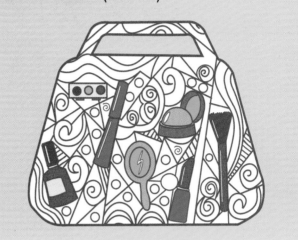

THE SWEET SMELL OF SUCCESS (PAGE 18)

Mostly As
You're a romantic girl who would suit a FLORAL perfume. Classic floral scents smell of just one flower, whereas more modern scents tend to combine a bouquet of several flowers. Think about which flower you most like the smell of before you go perfume shopping, then look for a perfume that matches.

Mostly Bs
You are a sporty girl who would suit an OCEANIC perfume with a clean, modern smell. This is a new category of perfume that only recently came on the market. Look for perfumes whose smell reminds you of freshly cut grass and the sea.

Mostly Cs
You are a confident girl who would suit a WOODY perfume. Woody perfumes suit free-spirited yet grounded girls who always know what they want. Look for scents that capture the essence of forests, the earth and woodlands.

Mostly Ds
You're a sophisticated girl who would suit a MUSK perfume. Look for a rich, heavy scent that has hints of vanilla, sumptuous flowers, and oriental spice.

THE FRIENDSHIP QUIZ (PAGE 28)

Mostly As
If ever one of your friends is feeling down, they know they can rely on you to cheer them up. You're the life and soul of every party, and love nothing more than having a giggle with your girlfriends. Make sure your friends know that you are there for them when they need to have a serious chat about things that are bothering them.

Mostly Bs
You're full of practical ideas and your friends always seek you out when they're looking for good advice. You're great at organising events and there's never a dull moment when you're around. Make sure you don't become too bossy.

Mostly Cs
You're a fantastic listener and love having long chats with close friends. Your friends know you'll always lend a sympathetic ear if they are having problems, and they value your friendship deeply. Don't forget to let your hair down and have fun occasionally.

DOING IT FOR THE WORLD (PAGE 32)

Mostly As
You're a super-green girl who's really doing her bit to help save the planet. Good work! As someone who understands the importance of looking after the world's resources, you should make it your mission to get as many other people as possible doing the same. Why not speak to your teachers about what could be done to make your school greener?

Mostly Bs
You're making an effort to help save the planet, and you know what needs to be done to make the world a greener place. Well done! There's still plenty of work to do, though, and you could start by making your house as green as possible. Sort out rotas and reminders so everyone who lives with you helps too.

Mostly Cs
You're just not the greenest girl in the world and could certainly do more to help preserve the planet's resources. Why not introduce one green thing into your life every month? You could start by switching your household to energy-saving light bulbs, and work up to growing your own food.

TERRIBLE TWINS (PAGE 30)

SHOPPING SPREE (PAGE 30)

GET TO SCHOOL (PAGE 41)

PARTY TIME (PAGE 45)

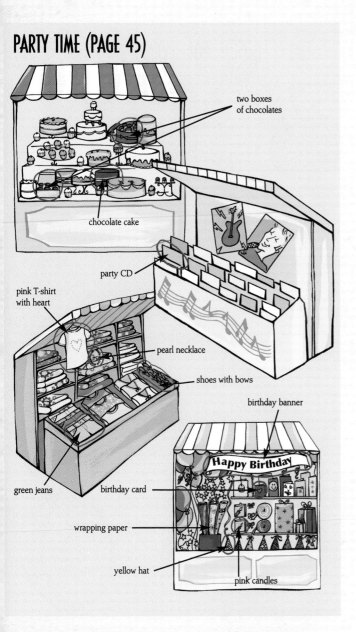

two boxes of chocolates

chocolate cake

party CD

pink T-shirt with heart

pearl necklace

shoes with bows

birthday banner

Happy Birthday

green jeans

birthday card

wrapping paper

yellow hat

pink candles

WHAT IS YOUR STORY? (PAGES 54 AND 55)

Mostly As

You have a fighting spirit and you approach life with the courage of a warrior. You're self-sufficient and never rely on other people to do things for you. Remember sometimes it's good to let your guard down and trust people – not everyone is out to get you.

Mostly Bs

You see the world as a beautiful place where people work together to do good things. You're kind, generous and thoughtful. Just make sure that people don't take advantage of your trusting nature.

Mainly Cs

You're a spiritual girl who believes that science can't explain everything that happens in the world. You're superstitious and like to surround yourself with good luck charms and healing crystals. Don't forget that sometimes it's important to take responsibility for your actions.

FAIRGROUND ATTRACTIONS (PAGES 52 AND 53)

CANDYFLOSS

There are ten sticks of candyfloss.

WHO'S DUCK?

A = 1, B = 5, C = 4, D = 2, E = 3